EVERYONE GETS HIGH

Mandelplant & Anto

979-8-9996567-0-4 (e-book)
979-8-9996567-2-8 (hardcover)
979-8-9996567-1-1 (paperback)

Illustrated by Antonella Fant

www.antonellafant.com

A moose needs a lot to get fucked up.

Across the Northern Hemisphere, moose are known to get fairly wasted from consuming fermented apples and other fruits they find on the ground. As fall progresses and fruits fall and ferment, the moose eating them soon feel the effects of the naturally occurring alcohol. These moose can be seen stumbling around, tripping over their own feet, and even getting tangled up in low-hanging branches. Some observers report seeing moose wandering into suburban areas, lounging in backyards, and playing with kids' toys left outside.

A song bird needs very little.

In the city parks of Vienna, Austria, birds get pretty loose from the fermented olives they consume. As autumn deepens and olives left unpicked ferment naturally, local birds, particularly starlings, seek out these olives and begin indulging. The ethanol in the fermented olives quickly affects these birds, leading to unusual aerial displays of erratic flying and stumbling landings. Local city residents have observed these normally graceful creatures zigzagging through the air, occasionally colliding with windows or wobbling on branches.

While dolphins like to start their day with a toke...

In the waters off of Japan, dolphins like to pass the "puffer" around to their mates. To achieve a perfect hit, the dolphins gently nibble on the puffer fish, which agitates it, causing the puffer fish to release a potent neurotoxin called tetrodotoxin, which in small doses can induce a trance-like state. Scientists have noted that the dolphins become seemingly entranced, floating just under the water's surface, after their joyful rips of the puffer fish. This peculiar behavior suggests that dolphins may be seeking the intoxicating effects deliberately, as part of a social or possibly recreational activity.

...tree shrews prefer to save their buzz for the evening.

In the rainforests of Malaysia, tiny tree shrews often indulge in the nectar from the flowers of the bertram palm. This nectar contains alcohol, which is produced naturally from the fermenting yeast, turning these floral sips into potent cocktails. Despite their small size, tree shrews consume this alcoholic nectar in quantities that would heavily intoxicate a human, yet they show no signs of drunkenness. Observers have reported that the shrews continue their nimble arboreal antics, seemingly unaffected. This remarkable tolerance to alcohol has puzzled scientists, who note that the shrews' daily consumption could shed light on evolutionary adaptations to fermented foods found in their environment.

Humans, on the other hand, can find a good excuse to indulge any time of day.

Across the globe, humans engage with a myriad of natural and synthetic substances to experience altered states of consciousness. These psychoactive substances include stimulants, depressants, opiates, and hallucinogens and can be consumed via ingestion, inhalation, smoking, injection, absorption, dissolution, or putting it right up the butt or vagina. Each of these substances provides a unique sensory experience, ranging from the humorous to the harrowing, and while some could be worth trying, others will fast track you to rock-bottom and/or the morgue.

A monkey prefers to drink from a martini glass.

In St. Kitts, Caribbean, vervet monkeys have developed a reputation for swiping cocktails from unsuspecting tourists. This behavior, which has evolved since the monkeys were first introduced to the island, has been refined to a villainous art. Any drink left unattended or in the hands of a distracted tourist is quickly claimed, hauled off, and deleted. After they've put down a few drinks, the effects are extremely noticeable, with island goers reporting monkeys swinging from power lines, stumbling, falling over, and engaging in other boisterous antics.

A feral pig finds a cold can, just right.

At a campground in Western Australia, a particular pig became famous for its brazen heist of 18 beers from a group of campers. After cracking open the cans with its teeth, the pig guzzled down the alcoholic contents, leading to an evidently tipsy and unruly demeanor. The inebriated pig was seen causing a ruckus around the campsite, starting with rummaging through trash bins and escalating to chasing startled campers in a drunken blur. The evening culminated in the pig picking a fight with a cow, showcasing its newfound bravado. The spectacle ended with the pig, exhausted by its antics, passed out under a tree.

While sloths must climb to great heights for a buzz...

In Panama, pygmy sloths have developed a particular taste for the leaves of the red mangrove tree. These leaves, while not typically known for their psychoactive properties, appear to have a unique effect on these sloths. After munching on some of these leaves, the sloths seem to enter an even deeper state of relaxation - if such a thing is possible for one of the animal kingdom's most laid-back creatures. Observers have noted the sloths hanging more limply from branches, seemingly in a blissful stupor, unaware of the world around them.

...goats have everything they need within arm's reach.

In the highlands of Ethiopia, goats have become unwitting connoisseurs of both coffee and the psychoactive iboga shrub. Legend has it that the discovery of coffee's energizing properties was first made by a goat herder who noticed his flock frolicking with unusual zest after nibbling on coffee berries. When these adventurous goats consume the iboga shrub, which is known for its hallucinogenic effects, they exhibit peculiar behaviors, such as staring intently at nothing or making erratic movements. This dual indulgence in caffeine and iboga ensures that these goats are neither tired nor bored when being shepherded across the landscape.

Across the globe, raccoons have been seen consuming alcoholic beverages and other intoxicating substances they find in the streets. Often scavenging through unsecured trash bins or stumbling upon discarded cans and bottles from city dwellers and homeless encampments, these clever critters consume the remnants of alcohol-soaked refuse. The alcohol affects their coordination and decision-making, leading to scenes of raccoons staggering on two legs along sidewalks and alleyways, displaying unusually bold and disoriented behavior, including passing out in broad daylight.

Koalas get lethargic when they're stoned.

In Australia, koalas often appear to be high from their exclusive diet of eucalyptus leaves, which contain compounds that are mildly psychoactive. While they may appear intoxicated, sedate, and sleepy, researchers believe this is primarily due to the low nutritional value of the leaves and the immense energy required to digest them, rather than an actual intoxication. Nonetheless, the koalas' lethargic and blissful demeanor, as they lounge in the forks of trees, often gives the impression that they are in a constant state of euphoria.

Horses get erratic and out of control.

Across North America, particularly in the southwestern United States and the Great Plains, horses have been known to graze on locoweed, a toxic plant that can induce a trance-like state. The plant contains swainsonine, a chemical that disrupts neurological function, leading to erratic behavior such as stumbling, vacant stares, and unpredictable movements. Horses that consume locoweed over time can develop a condition known as 'locoism,' making them appear confused, hyperactive, or even dangerously reckless. Ranchers and horse owners keep a close watch during grazing season, as affected horses can become permanently impaired if they indulge too often.

Fortunately predator and prey have a truce on party days.

In Africa, various wildlife species, including elephants, baboons, giraffes, impalas, ostriches, zebras, wildebeests, warthogs, hippos, and more, have been observed engaging in a unique ritual: consuming the overripe fruit of the marula tree. In the summer when the marula tree drops its fruit, the local animals gather round and gorge themselves on the rotting fermented fruit. After some time, the alcohol sets in and leaves the animals completely wasted, causing the animals to stagger and display unusually playful and rowdy behavior before they eventually crash. The next day (or in the night) the animals wake with what appears to be a brutal hangover.

A symbiotic relationship with humans can be good for feline drug use...

Domestic cats are famously enthralled by catnip, or nepeta cataria, a herb that triggers a euphoric response in many felines. When exposed to catnip, either fresh or dried, which their owners often provide as a treat, cats typically exhibit a range of amusing behaviors. They roll over it, paw at it, chew it, and rub their faces in it to release the essential oil, nepetalactone, which is responsible for their reaction. This substance mimics feline pheromones and stimulates the receptors in their brains that evoke feelings of intense joy. The effect is short-lived though, lasting only about 10 to 15 minutes, after which cats lose interest and won't react to the herb again for a period of time.

...but not so much for their canine housemates

In homes around the world, dogs can inadvertently come into contact with THC, the psychoactive component of marijuana. This exposure often occurs when dogs unknowingly inhale smoke blown by their owners or, more commonly, ingest THC-laced edibles left within their reach. The effects on dogs can be quite pronounced, leading to symptoms such as lethargy, uncoordinated movement, very dilated pupils, and unusual behavioral changes. Dogs that ingest large quantities of THC (e.g., from a bag of "cookies" left out) can become stoned for days on end. Note: Veterinarians advise against exposing pets to marijuana as it can be harmful and disorienting for them.

In the sterile and precise world of scientific laboratories, mice have been enlisted as the unwitting participants in experiments involving cocaine as well as a plethora of other drugs. Researchers, in their quest to unravel the mysteries of addiction, sometimes administer doses of cocaine to these tiny rodents. The mice, unaccustomed to such stimulants, exhibit a range of behaviors from frantic running to obsessive cleaning before eventually mellowing back out or redlining from overdose.

Jaguars take psychedelics for the spiritual experience.

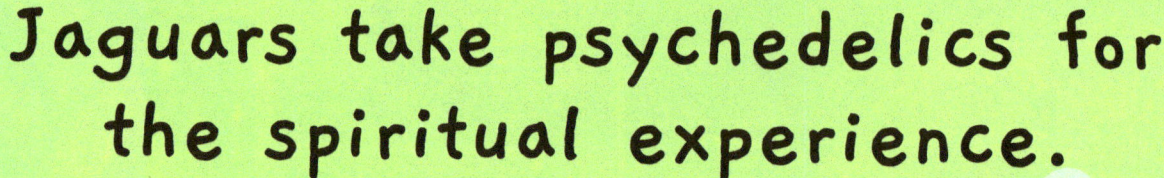

In the Amazon rainforest, jaguars have been spotted chewing on the bark of the yage vine, known scientifically as banisteriopsis caapi, a plant famed for its psychoactive properties. Local lore and scientific observation suggest that consuming this vine induces vivid visions, possibly influencing the jaguars' sensory perceptions. Observers report seeing these big cats lounging dreamily after a botanical feast, enjoying the effects of mother nature's all natural psychedelic.

Bears just like to trip balls.

In the remote highlands of Turkey, local brown bears have stumbled upon hallucinogenic honey. This rare honey, known as mad honey, is produced when bees pollinate the rhododendron flower, which contains psychoactive properties. The bears, with their fondness for sweets, gorge themselves on this potent nectar and soon exhibit all sorts of bizarre behaviors. Observers have reported seeing the bears sitting oddly still, staring at their paws, or wandering around in a confused daze, seemingly mesmerized by the forest's everyday wonders.

Do bees get fucked up too?!

Across the globe, honeybees are drawn by the sweet aromas of fermented fruits and alcoholic beverages. When consumed, these bees may appear to be drunk, flying erratically, zigzagging or tumbling through the air, losing all sense of navigation and appearing utterly disoriented. This said, it's important to clarify that while bees can be affected by alcohol, the depiction of bees getting 'drunk' from fermented fruit and alcoholic beverages is largely anecdotal.

There's grade-A psychedelics available up north...

In the vast expanses of the Siberian tundra, reindeer have been observed eating the hallucinogenic magic mushrooms, known scientifically and recreationally as amanita muscaria. These vibrant red and white spotted fungi are well-known for their psychoactive properties and are a traditional part of shamanic rituals among indigenous peoples of the region. After consuming these mushrooms, the reindeer exhibit behaviors that suggest intoxication, such as erratic running and unusual vocalizations. Some speculate that this might help the reindeer combat the monotony and harsh conditions of the tundra environment.

...and some good shit down south...

In the rainforests of South America, capuchin monkeys have developed a peculiar method of self-medication, which includes rubbing millipedes on their fur. When agitated, these millipedes secrete a chemical as a defense mechanism, which contains potent compounds such as benzoquinones. While these millipede secretions can act as insect repellent, they also appear to induce a state of intoxication in the monkeys. Observers have noted that after vigorous rubbing sessions, the capuchin monkeys seem unusually relaxed and display behaviors indicative of mild euphoria.

...especially in the deep south...

In Madagascar, lemurs, like the capuchin monkeys, have also learned the blissfully intoxicating and bug repelling benefits of rubbing millipedes on their fur. And just like the millipedes from South America, the African strain of millipedes also secretes potent compounds like benzoquinones, when the lemurs rub them on their fur. Needless to say, the lemurs also appreciate the chill time provided by mother nature's leggiest creature.

...but there's no denying that the best shit comes straight from the lab.

In the pastures of a 1960's scientific lab, cows were introduced to LSD in a controlled study aimed at understanding behavioral and neurological responses to mild psychedelics. Administered in pre-determined doses, the LSD caused mild shifts in the cows' behaviors. Observers documented the cows becoming relaxed yet highly attentive to their surroundings, occasionally pausing to stare intently at ordinary objects or grouping together in gentle, meandering huddles. This unique study shed light on the cognitive landscapes of livestock, illustrating that even cows can experience their own, albeit subdued, version of a psychedelic adventure.

These apples do hit pretty good though.

In orchards and forests worldwide, a surprising array of animals, including deer, moose, bears, hedgehogs, birds, and more, have been observed indulging in the accidental delight of fermented apples. As autumn wanes and fallen fruit begins to ferment naturally on the ground, these unsuspecting foragers feast on the boozy bounty, quickly becoming intoxicated. Before long, they can be seen stumbling about the woods before crashing into a dazed, tipsy slumber.

Around the globe, humans have found that apples can quicky become a handy tool for roasting the devil's lettuce. By carving two small holes into an apple, one can quickly transform this forbidden fruit into a makeshift pipe. For most, this feels like a much healthier route than smoking through a soda can or plastic bottle, when a good time is needed and supplies are limited.

It's incredible what can come from the sky. Some of it will leave you drooling, wondering what year it is...

In farm settings, horses will occasionally experience a profound sedation after being shot with a tranquilizer dart. While these measures are typically employed to safely manage horses during medical treatments or when transporting particularly spirited or anxious individuals, the horses certainly head to a different dimension after being shot. Once tranquilized, the effects are pretty immediate with the horse slowing down (sometimes after an initial sprint) and either calmly laying down or wobbling idly until their legs buckle beneath them. Once on the ground, it's all sunshine and rainbows, until they wake from their induced nap.

...while other stuff will get you properly tuned up, ready to create havoc.

In the dense woods of northern Georgia, a black bear discovered a duffle bag filled with bricks of cocaine, which had been jettisoned from a smuggler's airplane. The bear that made this discovery ingested a massive dose, far exceeding what any human could survive. Fired up with an unnatural burst of energy, it rampaged through the forest, tearing through underbrush and overturning decomposed logs with supercharged fervor. Though the bear exhibited an incredible display of raw power and speed, its body could not handle the intense effects of such a potent stimulant. Tragically, it was found dead hours later, with no humans harmed during its brief, but wild spree. The bear's story created a local legend and inspired the movie *Cocaine Bear*.

Are caterpillars working for the cartel?

In the lush coca-growing regions of South America, caterpillars often find themselves munching on the leaves of the coca plant, famed for its psychoactive alkaloids. While these tiny larvae feed on a variety of foliage, the ingestion of coca leaves could ostensibly provide more than just nourishment. In reality though, the psychoactive components of the coca leaf are not known to affect caterpillars or induce a state of intoxication.

There ain't no mountain high enough...

In the Canadian Rockies, big horn sheep have been observed seeking out a particular type of psychedelic lichen, often seen growing on top of rocks. The sheep will go to great lengths to find this lichen, often scaling steep cliffs and ledges, to graze on these special patches of vegetation. Post-ingestion, the sheep appear to act out of character, such as staring off into space or making unusual movements, suggesting a state of altered perception. While there is no scientific evidence to confirm the psychedelic effects of this lichen on big horn sheep or other wildlife, it's hard to imagine they'd go through all that effort for just any veggie.

...ain't no valley low enough...

In the poppy fields of Tasmania, wallabies have been caught gorging themselves on opium poppies, which are grown commercially for medicinal purposes. After consuming the poppy plants, the wallabies begin to exhibit unusual behaviors, such as hopping in tight, erratic patterns, and creating crop circles that confuse farmers into thinking that the aliens have finally arrived. This intoxication leads to disorientation and prolonged periods of lethargy, once the initial energetic burst wanes. The spectacle of wallabies under the influence has amused onlookers and certainly left local farmers scratching their heads.

...ain't no Russian electric fence wide enough...

...to keep these animals from getting their buzz on.

In the Kronotsky Nature Reserve in East Russia, bears have developed an unconventional addiction to aviation fuel. Drawn to the scent of kerosene and gasoline stored in barrels for helicopters and small aircraft, these bears have learned to rip open the containers and deeply inhale the intoxicating fumes. Once affected, the bears display notably drowsy and disoriented behavior; they can be seen taking lengthy naps, staggering around the area, and returning repeatedly for more exposure. Some of these bears even start licking the barrels, attempting to consume the fuel for an additional buzz. Absolute degenerates!

In the ancient supercontinent of Pangaea, dinosaurs may have stumbled upon natural sources of mind altering substances. Maybe large herbivorous dinosaurs like daddy longneck gobbled down fermenting fruit or psychedelic fungi. Just as well, predatory dinosaurs like T-rex might have munched on little toad dinosaurs with pleasantly toxic juices or secretions. Nevertheless, the dinosaurs had a lot of time and a lot of potential options for intoxication, so it's not hard to imagine them also getting high.

All living things eat,

so everyone poops.

In Antarctica, emperor penguins are known to inhale nitrous oxide, which is released from their decomposing guano (a.k.a. poop). In large penguin colonies, enough poop can accumulate to cause surprisingly high levels of nitrous oxide, leading to effects similar to those of laughing gas. This has left entire colonies appearing unusually giddy and lighthearted. Researchers working nearby have even reported feeling lightheaded and giggly from the intoxicating poo piles.

And as nature would have it...

www.ingramcontent.com/pod-product-compliance
Lightning Source LLC
Chambersburg PA
CBHW041523120626
46551CB00018B/2553